LOL

VALENTINE'S

DAY

JOKES

FOR KIDS

Did you hear about the two centipedes in love?

They would complete each others centi-ses.

 What candy is only for girls?

HER-SHEy's Kisses.

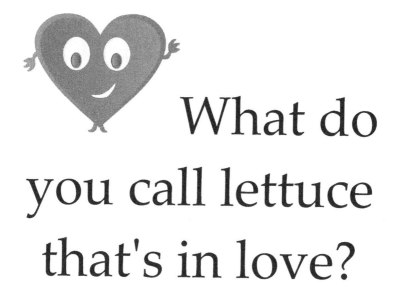 What do you call lettuce that's in love?

Head over heels.

What kind of fruit do calendars love?

Dates!

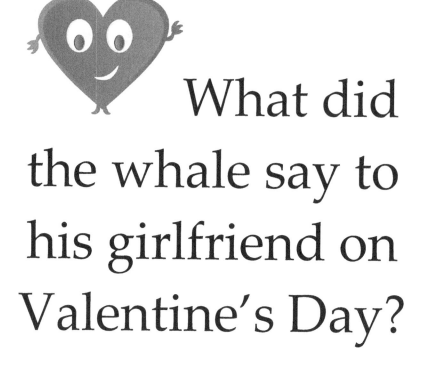 What did the whale say to his girlfriend on Valentine's Day?

"Whale you be mine?"

 What did one beet say to the other on Valentine's Day?

"You make my heart beet faster!"

 What happened when the magicians went on a date?

It was love at first slight.

 What do cars do at the Valentine's Day party?

Brake dance

What's the best thing about Valentine's Day?

The day after when all the chocolate goes on sale!

 Why didn't the skeleton break up with his girlfriend on Valentine's Day?

He didn't have the heart!

 What do squirrels give for Valentine's Day?

Forget-me-nuts.

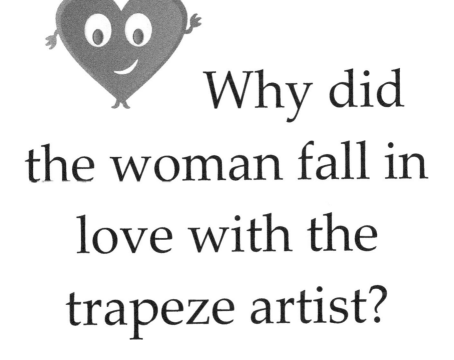 Why did the woman fall in love with the trapeze artist?

Because of his net worth.

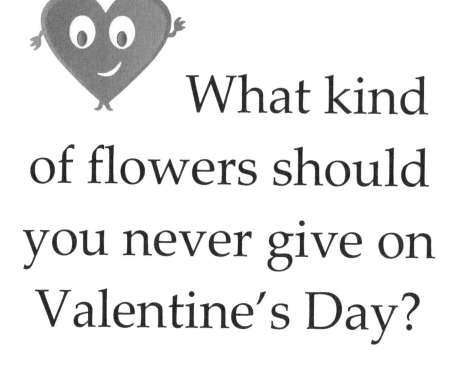 What kind of flowers should you never give on Valentine's Day?

Cauliflowers.

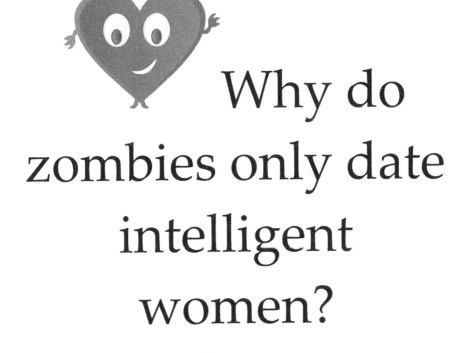 Why do zombies only date intelligent women?

They just love a woman with BRAAAINS!

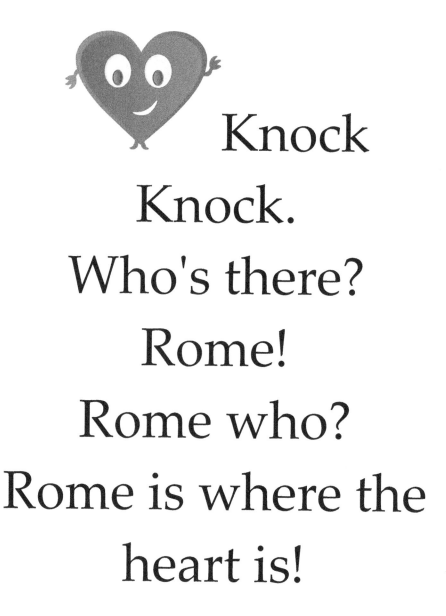

Knock
Knock.
Who's there?
Rome!
Rome who?
Rome is where the
heart is!

 What do Valentine's Day flowers call their best friends?

Buds.

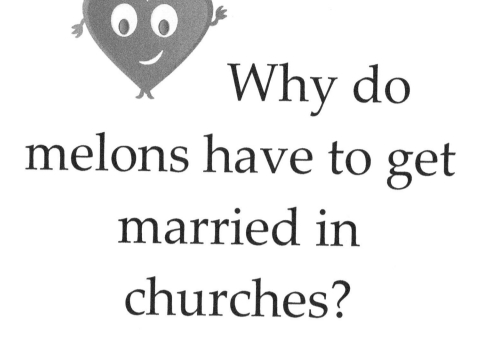 Why do melons have to get married in churches?

Because they cantaloupe!

 Why do
oars fall in love?

Because they're
row-mantic.

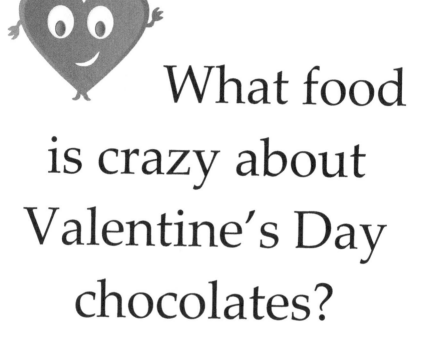 What food is crazy about Valentine's Day chocolates?

A cocoa-nut.

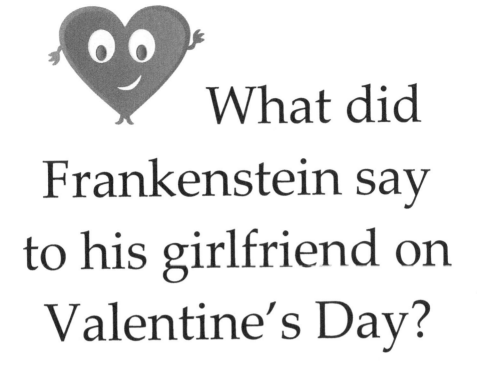 What did Frankenstein say to his girlfriend on Valentine's Day?

Be my Valen-stein!

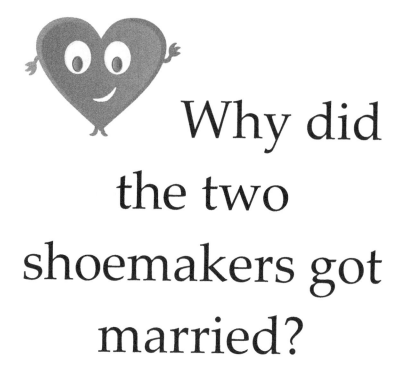 Why did the two shoemakers got married?

Because they were sole mates.

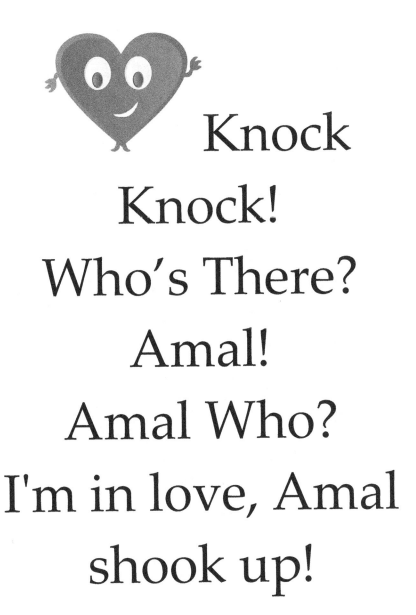

Knock
Knock!
Who's There?
Amal!
Amal Who?
I'm in love, Amal
shook up!

What did Pilgrims give each other on Valentine's Day?

Mayflowers.

 What happened when the woman stole the policeman's heart?

He did a cardiac arrest.

 Two antennae met on a roof, fell in love and got married. Their wedding ceremony wasn't fancy. The reception, however, was excellent!

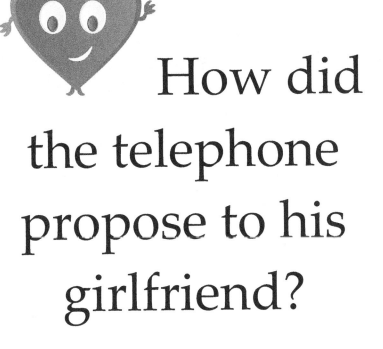 How did the telephone propose to his girlfriend?

He gave her a ring.

 What did
the painter say to
her boyfriend?

"I love you with
all my art!"

 What did the husband get his wife on Valentine's Day to take her breath away?

A treadmill.

What did the Mr. Mentos say to Mrs. Mentos?

"It's Valentine's Day and we're mint for each other."

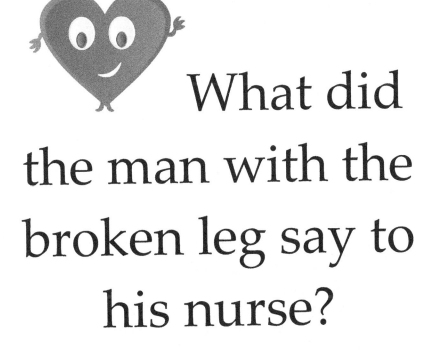 What did the man with the broken leg say to his nurse?

"I've got a crutch on you!"

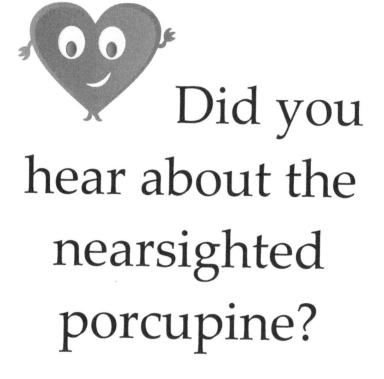 Did you hear about the nearsighted porcupine?

He fell in love with a pincushion!

 Where does spaghetti go on Valentine's Day?

The meat ball!

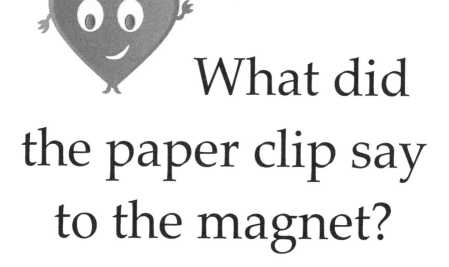 What did the paper clip say to the magnet?

"I find you super attractive!"

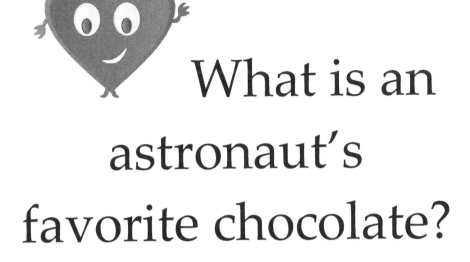 What is an astronaut's favorite chocolate?

A Milky Way!

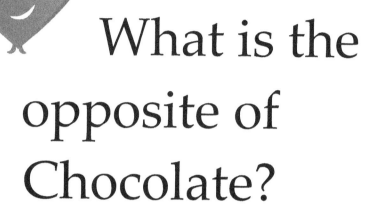 What is the opposite of Chocolate?

Choco-early.

 What do you get when you dip a kitten in chocolate?

A Kitty Kat bar!

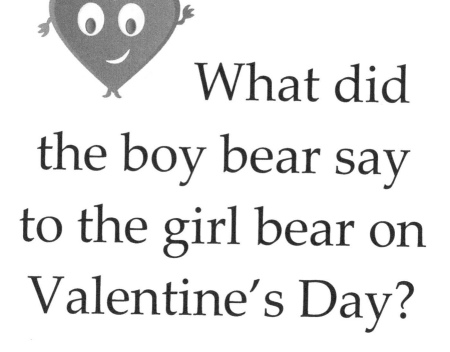 What did the boy bear say to the girl bear on Valentine's Day?

"I love you beary much!"

 Why is Valentine's Day the best day for a celebration?

Because you can really party hearty!

What did the recently reunited girlfriend say to her boyfriend on a foggy Valentine's Day?

"I mist you."

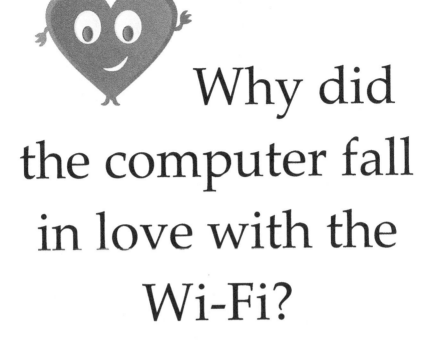 Why did the computer fall in love with the Wi-Fi?

They just had a connection.

 What happens when two single buffalo meet up, fall in love and run away to get married?

They buffalope!

 What did the French chef give his wife for Valentine's Day?

A hug and a quiche.

 What do you call a very small valentine?

A valen-tiny!

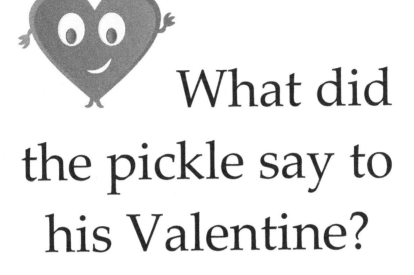 What did the pickle say to his Valentine?

"You mean a great *dill* to me."

What did
one volcano say to
the other on
Valentine's Day?

I lava you.

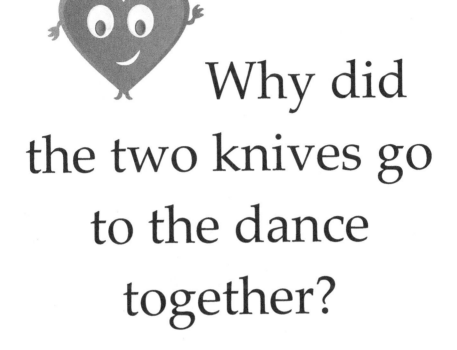 Why did the two knives go to the dance together?

Because they both looked sharp!

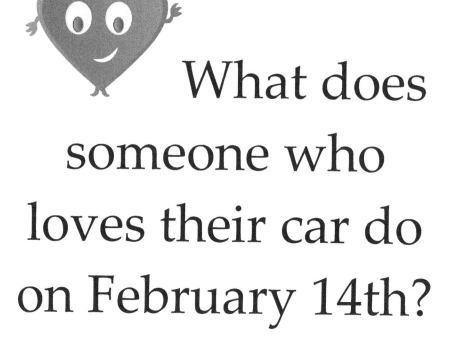 What does someone who loves their car do on February 14th?

They give it a valen-shine!

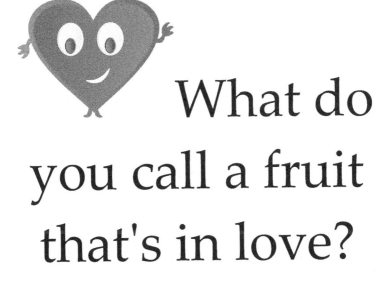 What do
you call a fruit
that's in love?

Peachy-Keen

What is the best thing to put on Valentine's Day chocolate?

Your teeth.

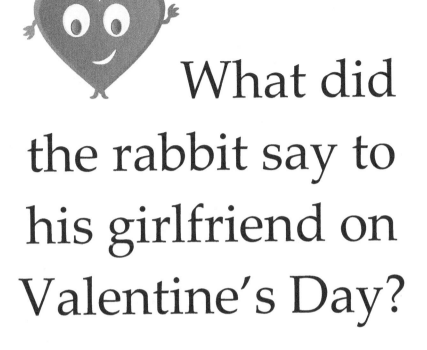 What did the rabbit say to his girlfriend on Valentine's Day?

"Some bunny wuvs you!"

Knock Knock.
Who's there?
Pauline!
Pauline Who?
I think I'm Pauline
in love with you.

Design A Valentine

Design A Valentine

Design A Valentine

Design A Valentine

Design A Valentine

Design A Valentine

Made in the USA
Middletown, DE
07 February 2020